FIRST
PEOPLES
OF NORTH
AMERICA

THE PEOPLE AND CULTURE OF THE
CHOCTAW

SAMANTHA NEPHEW
RAYMOND BIAL

Cavendish
Square

New York

Published in 2017 by Cavendish Square Publishing, LLC
243 5th Avenue, Suite 136, New York, NY 10016

Library of Congress Cataloging-in-Publication Data

Names: Nephew, Samantha, author. | Bial, Raymond, author.
Title: The people and culture of the Choctaw / Samantha Nephew and Raymond Bial.
Description: New York : Cavendish Square Publishing, [2017] | Series: First peoples of North America | Includes bibliographical references and index.
Identifiers: LCCN 2016029167 | ISBN 9781502622457 (library bound) | ISBN 9781502622464 (eBook)
Subjects: LCSH: Choctaw Indians--History--Juvenile literature. | Choctaw Indians--Social life and customs--Juvenile literature.
Classification: LCC E99.C8 N47 2017 | DDC 976.004/97387--dc23
LC record available at https://lccn.loc.gov/2016029167

Editorial Director: David McNamara
Editor: Kristen Susienka
Copy Editor: Rebecca Rohan
Associate Art Director/Designer: Amy Greenan
Production Coordinator: Karol Szymczuk
Photo Research: J8 Media

ACKNOWLEDGMENTS

From Samantha Nephew: I acknowledge the lives and memories of Arthur and Zenna Nephew of Buffalo, New York. Art and Zenna showed me by example how to love and care for community, how to honor our heritage, and stand up for what's right. They continue to be a guiding light even today. I would also like to thank the Seneca Nation of Indians—I've been given many opportunities to thrive thanks to the care this Nation gives to its enrolled members. Cultural preservation is strong within the Nation and allows me the opportunity to learn about and keep our heritage alive despite its relatively small membership of about 8,000. To my husband, Mark James. For your years of support, love, and confidence in my abilities—even when I wasn't so sure. I like you. My family, Shelby Nephew, Cassie Bradley, the entire Ledsome family, Aunt Sue, and Grandma Deanna. And to those who've helped and encourage me unconditionally: Natalie Rodriguez, Jennifer Castro, Johnnie Fenderson, Jennifer Mecozzi, Megan Connelly, and Jennifer Heisel.

From Raymond Bial: This book would not have been possible without the generous help of many individuals and organizations that have dedicated themselves to honoring the customs of the Choctaw. I would like to thank in particular Cavendish Square Publishing and all who contributed to finding photos and other materials for publication. Finally, I would like to thank my family and friends for their constant support along this writing journey.

CONTENTS

A young Choctaw woman performs a traditional dance.

AUTHORS' NOTE

At the dawn of the twentieth century, Native Americans were thought to be a vanishing race. However, despite four hundred years of warfare, deprivation, and disease, Native people have not gone away. Countless millions have lost their lives, but over the course of this century the populations of Native tribes have grown tremendously. Even as Native people struggle to adapt to modern Western life, they have also kept the flame of their traditions alive—the language, religion, stories, and the everyday ways of life. An exhilarating renaissance in Native American culture is now sweeping the nation from coast to coast.

The First Peoples of North America books depict the social and cultural life of the major nations, from the early history of Native peoples in North America to their present-day struggles for survival, dignity, and to preserve their cultures. Historical and contemporary photographs of traditional subjects, as well as period illustrations, are blended throughout each book so that readers may gain a sense of family life in a tipi, a hogan, a longhouse, or in houses today.

No single book can comprehensively portray the intricate and varied lifeways of an entire tribe, or nation. We only hope that young people will come away with a deeper appreciation for the rich tapestry of Native culture—both then and now—and a keen desire to learn more about these first Americans.

Choctaw member
Bertram Bobb tells
stories of his uncle
and cousin.

CHAPTER ONE

Returning to source is stillness, which is the way of nature. Each separate being in the universe returns to the common source for serenity, to replenish the soul, which enables them to grow and flourish .

—Rhonda Redbird
(Choctaw, Cherokee)

A CULTURE BEGINS

Native Americans have had a long history. Although their exact origins are yet to be agreed upon, many speculate the first people came to North America during an ice age, migrating from Asia into Alaska and dispersing to other regions over many generations. Regardless of exact origin, eventually groups of people populated North America and formed tribes. Each tribe has its own origin story, and each tribe has uniquely contributed to the history of North America. One such group is the Choctaw.

The Choctaw Begin

The **Choctaw** (CHOK-taw) have had a rich past. They were one of the largest tribes of the Southeast. These tribes included the Creek, Chickasaw, and Seminole. A peaceful, farming people, the Choctaw generally enjoyed good relations with their neighbors. Although the Choctaw had no written language for centuries, their heritage was passed down over the generations through a technique called oral tradition. People learned the art of making handicrafts and how to play games, as well as how to speak the Choctaw language and important Choctaw stories and beliefs.

Among the many stories told by the Choctaw are legends that trace their origin to a distant country in the Northwest. Some say that the people followed a medicine man who carried a sacred pole. According to others, the tribes were led by two brothers, Chahta and Chikasa, who brought the people to a **mound** called **Nanih Waiya**. Chahta and his followers stayed near this "mother mound" and became the Choctaw tribe, while Chikasa and his group wandered off, becoming the Chickasaw tribe. Still other stories tell of the Choctaw emerging from Nanih Waiya, near the headwaters of the Pearl River in the center of present-day Mississippi. The name of the state and the great river comes from the Choctaw *Misha sipokni*, which aptly means "older than time." Here is one version of the legend of a medicine man and the sacred pole:

Many winters ago, the Choctaw embarked on a long journey eastward from a distant land in the Northwest. No one is certain of the location of this country, only that it was far to the west of the wide Mississippi River and the high, snow-topped peaks of the Rocky Mountains.

Led by a wise and powerful medicine man, the Choctaw traveled for many years. Each day, the medicine man went forward with a red pole. Each night when the people camped, he thrust the pole in the ground. Every morning, he found that the pole was leaning to the east. He told the people that they would continue eastward. The medicine man explained that the Great Spirit was guiding them to a new home. They would know when to end their wandering and where to settle when the pole remained straight up.

One day, the Choctaw came to a mound known as Nanih Waiya. Again, as he did every evening, the medicine man stuck the pole into the ground. They camped there that night. When they awoke in the morning, the pole was not tilting eastward—it was standing upright. At last, the Great Spirit had shown the Choctaw where to make their new home. Here they settled, and Nanih Waiya stands at the heart of the Choctaw Nation to this very day.

The People and Culture of the Choctaw

Nanih Waiya is a sacred Choctaw mound.

Forming a Society

Like the other Native peoples of North America, the ancestors of the Choctaw formed functioning, thriving communities over generations. Typically, the women gathered roots, berries, and seeds, while the men hunted in the shadowy forests and fished in the sparkling rivers. During the winter, small groups of men went on bear hunts, moving quietly through the mist, in the soggy bottomlands. In early spring, some of the more daring young men ventured westward across the Mississippi River to pursue the vast herds of bison (often called buffalo) grazing on the southern Great Plains. In large fields around their villages, they planted corn, squash, beans, and other crops.

With a population of about twenty thousand people, the Choctaw—traditionally known to other Native peoples as the **Chata**—formed a confederacy, or union, of villages. They dominated a vast territory of more than 23 million acres (9.3 million hectares) in what is now Mississippi and parts of Alabama and Louisiana. For many centuries, they lived in more than one hundred villages, journeying only to hunt large game and trade with other tribes.

The Choctaw encountered people of European descent around 1540, when Spanish explorer Hernando de Soto wandered into their territory. Over time, the tribes of the Southeast, including the Choctaw, formed a tumultuous relationship with the French, who sought to dominate the region. Later, the Choctaw entered into trade relations with the British and became embroiled in the North American conflicts of the European powers. The Choctaw also had to deal with American settlers pushing into their territory. These encounters with Europeans drastically changed their way of life. By the mid-1830s, many Choctaw had been forced to give up their homelands and move many miles away to **Indian Territory** in what is now Oklahoma. The word "Oklahoma" comes from a Choctaw term *Okla-humma*, which means "Red People." Others hid out in Mississippi, where they struggled to survive in the forests.

A People of the Land

Prior to the influence of Europeans, the Choctaw enjoyed the South's mild winters with little ice and snow, and hot, humid summers. However, the weather could also become quite intense, even destructive. Storms frequently swept over the land, throwing down curtains of drenching rain and generating tornadoes that tore across the landscape. During the winter, traces of snow might fall in the northern reaches of their territory, while in the late summer and early fall, hurricanes occasionally swirled up from the Gulf of Mexico, slamming the southern coastline.

The rolling hills were blanketed with deep, green forests, which extended north to what is now the state of Tennessee, east into Alabama and Georgia, and west to the Mississippi River. The Gulf of Mexico featured warm breezes and sandy beaches. The coastline, which featured lovely bays, was shielded from the Gulf of Mexico by the shallow Mississippi Sound. The coast was also partly enclosed and protected by a string

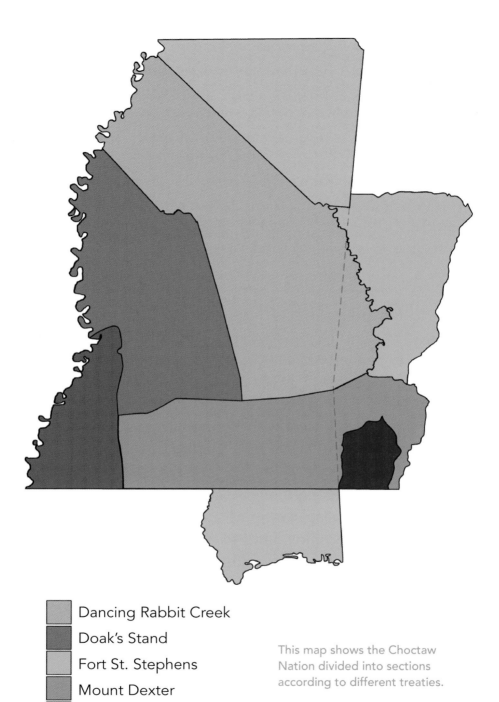

Dancing Rabbit Creek

Doak's Stand

Fort St. Stephens

Mount Dexter

Hoe Buckintoopa

Fort Adams

This map shows the Choctaw Nation divided into sections according to different treaties.

The People and Culture of the Choctaw

of islands—Petit Bois, Horn, Ship, and Cat Islands—located several miles from the shore.

Woodall Mountain in northeast Mississippi reached just over 800 feet (244 meters) into the sky, but much of the Choctaw's traditional homeland was relatively low and flat. The territory was mostly shaped by water—the coastal plain of the Gulf of Mexico and the floodplain of the Mississippi River. Toward the east, the coastal plain was composed of low hills, including the Pine Hills. Toward the northeast, the elevations rose slightly at the Pontotoc Ridge and the Fall Line Hills.

The soils in which the Choctaw planted corn, beans, and squash ranged from the light brown loam of the forests to the black earth of the prairie land. Located in the eastern part of their territory, this fertile prairie is now known as the Black Belt. At first, the Choctaw carved fields out of the thick forest, but they came to plant crops in the rich soil of the Black Belt as well.

The Choctaw Homelands

The Choctaw territory was laced with many creeks and rivers, most notably the Mississippi River, with the Yazoo and Big Black Rivers as the major tributaries. Winding through the heart of Choctaw country, the Pearl, Pascagoula, and Tombigbee Rivers flowed south to the Gulf of Mexico. The region was also dotted with marshes, swamps, and lakes, including many oxbow lakes caused by changes in the meandering course of the rivers. When the river cuts a new, shorter channel through the curve, it leaves a loop as a separate oxbow-shaped lake. In the twentieth and twenty-first

The People and Culture of the Choctaw

centuries, many of the rivers were dammed to form huge lakes, notably the Ross Barnett Reservoir on the Pearl River, not far from the current Choctaw reservation in Mississippi.

At one time, most of the land was covered with forests, and the Choctaw used the trees for firewood and building materials for their houses. In the northern part of their territory, hardwoods such as elm, hickory, and oak, along with cedar, shortleaf pine, and tupelo grew in abundance. Further south, loblolly, longleaf, and slash pines flourished in the rolling hills. There were also live oak, magnolia, pecan, and sweet gum trees. In the spring, the dogwoods blossomed, along with other flowering plants—azaleas, irises, silver bell, sweetbell, trillium, and violets. The Choctaw gathered plants for food and medicine, and hunted game, such as white-tailed deer and bear. They also caught small animals such as fox, beavers, opossums, skunks, rabbits, and squirrels. Men hunted quail and wild turkeys, and in the wetlands, egrets, herons, and terns. They fished for black bass, catfish, and perch in the freshwater streams and caught saltwater fish, crabs, oysters, and shrimp in the coastal waters.

The homeland of the Choctaw also encompassed sacred places, notably Nanih Waiya. Mentioned in nearly every version of the Choctaw origin story, Nanih Waiya has figured prominently in Choctaw history. It is believed that the Choctaw built the earthen mound between 1,500 and 2,000 years ago to mark the end of their long migration. Erected over at least two or three generations, Nanih Waiya was likely also the site of a religious temple. Like other mounds in the Southeast, Nanih Waiya has a slightly flat top. It rises about 25 feet (7.6 m) above the surrounding land. Oblong in shape, the mound spreads over less than 1 acre (0.4 ha) of land. Nanih Waiya was abandoned sometime after the first European explorers ventured into the region. Today, the mound is revered by the Choctaw.

Despite enduring many hardships, the Choctaw have continued to make their home in this beloved land for generations, and they prosper today in reservation communities scattered throughout Neshoba County in east central Mississippi.

Forests and lakes dotted Choctaw territory.

A portrait of Chief Mushalatubbee, circa 1834

CHAPTER TWO

If you feel that our world seems to be spiritually connecting, that's because we are.

—A. Peerless (Choctaw woman)

BUILDING A CIVILIZATION

The first Choctaw people developed ways of life, including housing, meals, and games. They formed a civilization that flourished for centuries without European or other outside influences.

Life in a Choctaw Village

The Choctaw lived in small, scattered towns, most of which were situated in three geographic regions, or districts. The villages of the Okla Falaya, or Tall People, were located primarily around the upper Pearl River, along the western edge of the confederacy. The Okla Tannap, or

This painting by Francois Bernard shows a Choctaw village.

People of the Other Side, lived in an area just west of the Tombigbee River in the eastern part of Choctaw territory. The Okla Hannali, or Six Town People, settled around the upper Chickasawhay River in the southern part of the territory. For generations, most of the Choctaw made their home within one of these three areas. Each group varied slightly in language and dress and developed its own trade relations with neighboring tribes: the Okla Falaya with the Chickasaw in the north, the Okla Tannap with the Creeks in the east, and the Okla Hannali with the tribes to the south along Mobile Bay.

Government

A **Mingo**, or principal chief, governed each of the three districts. A man who had proven his ability as a leader was chosen by the other men for this position. A Mingo

The People and Culture of the Choctaw

usually came from a prominent family. Each town also had its own leader, or peace chief, and a council of elders to advise him. The town leader also had four or five aides who helped him address daily situations and plan for the future. Men were often consulted for their wisdom and experience in managing the everyday affairs of the town. They also played a prominent role in ceremonies. The Choctaw, who were warriors of great prowess, also had war chiefs. The war chiefs wielded considerable authority during warfare and diplomatic negotiations. Responsible for all military concerns, the war chief was usually chosen from one of the aides to the town leader.

When a major issue arose that affected everyone in the area, the Mingo convened a council of all the town leaders in the region. The Mingos of each region also jointly governed the entire Choctaw Nation. On occasion, the three Mingos convened a large council of all the members of the councils of all the regions. Everyone had a right to speak at these meetings, and decisions were made democratically by majority vote. The Choctaw became well known for their participatory government—at all levels. Their government emphasized free speech. They often held public meetings under the cool shade of a large brush arbor. However, a hole was left in the center of the roof. Anyone who wished to speak had to stand beneath the opening, in the intense rays of the sun or the harsh blowing wind, rain, or occasional snow. In the heat and humidity, people usually did not speak too long. Yet the Choctaw spoke well and were reputed to be great orators.

The Choctaw built some of their dwellings, like this storehouse, on poles.

Choctaw society was also organized into two moieties, or sections, that each included six to eight **clans**, or *iksas*. Each person was born into a clan, which is similar to a large, extended family. Clans of both moieties lived and worked together in each Choctaw community. When it was time to marry, a man or woman took a partner from one of the clans of the opposite moiety. Choctaw society was **matrilineal**, meaning that people traced their descent through a common female ancestor. Babies were born into their mother's clan, while the father remained a member of the clan of his mother. Although they did not hold official leadership positions, women exercised a great deal of influence within Choctaw society.

Villages and Houses

Choctaw towns could have as many as three hundred houses. The towns also included several public buildings, notably the council house and storage buildings. An open space among the buildings served as a town square. Here, dances and other religious ceremonies were held. Towns were often enclosed with palisades of sharpened logs. The Choctaw sometimes dug moats around the town, an additional defense against enemy attack.

The Choctaw lived in two kinds of dwellings—a summer and a winter home. Each home was built by placing wooden poles in the ground and lashing them together to form a round frame. These houses were known as wattle and daub houses, or sometimes

Traditional Choctaw winter houses

chickees. Summer homes were sheathed with mats of woven reeds. Raising the mats allowed cool breezes to flow through the dwelling. The walls of winter homes were plastered with mud and covered with cypress or pine bark. Both types of houses had thatched roofs to shed the rain. A hole in the roof let out the smoke rising from the fire in the center of the earthen floor. The windowless buildings had one door, which usually faced south. The door was only about 3 or 4 feet (0.9 to 1.2 m) high so that people had to stoop when they entered or exited.

Large enough to shelter one or two families, homes were simply furnished. People slept on beds raised on poles 3 or 4 feet (0.9 or 1.2 m) from the ground. The beds were covered with mats and animal skins. People often used buffalo skins as blankets. Other belongings—clothing, baskets, clay pots, cooking utensils, tools, and weapons—were kept in the home. These household items and the home itself belonged to the women of the family.

The Choctaw had a rich culture and civilization that drew from the landscape and the world around them. From their surroundings they were able to develop methods of survival and prosper.

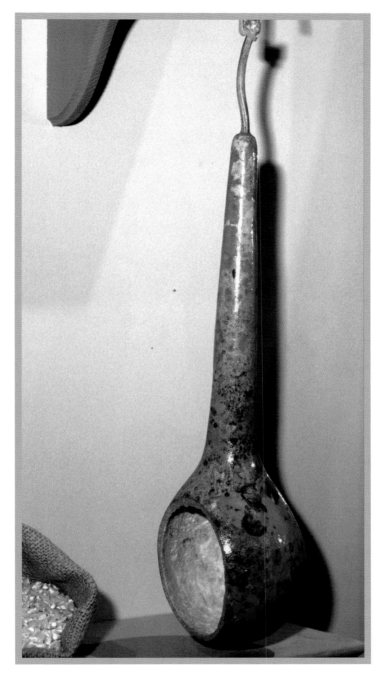

The Choctaw used the world around them to create tools. Here, a ladle was made from a gourd.

A Choctaw family,
circa 1910

CHAPTER THREE

To watch us dance is to watch our hearts speak.

—Hopi/Choctaw proverb

LIFE IN THE CHOCTAW NATION

The Choctaw Nation drew together men, women, and children. Each member of the community contributed equally to their society, and each village celebrated deeply rooted traditions from birth to death.

Family Roles

Choctaw family members had their own traditional roles and responsibilities.

Grandparents often lived with their children's families. They were respected as tribal elders and often consulted for their wisdom. They told stories and undertook important duties, such as presenting the bride at weddings and helping to look after the children. Along with caring for their children and homes, mothers also tended large fields shared by everyone in the town. They also undertook the tasks of storing food and preparing meals for their families. They tanned deer and buffalo hides and made them into clothing. They wove reeds and canes into baskets and shaped clay into useful pots. Men served as hunters and warriors, as well as tribal leaders, traders, and medicine men. They also caught fish, cleared fields, built houses, and crafted weapons, tools, and canoes.

The Life Cycle

The Choctaw saw the cycle of life from birth to death as sacred. They had ceremonies and celebrations associated with each stage of life. Here are a few examples of their traditions.

Menstruation and Birth

Whenever a woman had her period, she left her home. Camping outside the town, she lit a fire. If she took fire with her, it was believed that her home would be polluted. During this time, men had to prepare their own meals or eat with their neighbors. Similarly, when a woman was about to give birth, she went into the woods by herself. Near the time of delivery, her husband ate only after sunset, and if his wife gave birth to a girl, he observed this fast for eight more days. She usually gave birth without any assistance. She washed the baby herself and placed the newborn, who was not swathed or otherwise bound in clothing, in a cradle made of cane. She soon returned to her work at home and in the town. Mothers nursed their babies until they were three or four years of age, or even older. It was not uncommon for children to say to their mothers, "Sit down so that I may nurse."

A painting of a Choctaw ball game

Growing Up

Parents raised their children in a loving but careful manner. Children were encouraged to run freely, so they would be fast and strong. Boys and girls were expected to do chores, such as fetching water and hauling firewood. With their mothers, they gathered nuts and berries in the forests and fields. Taught to be hardworking and generous, children were told that little spirits would kidnap them if they misbehaved or did not finish their work. From their mothers and older sisters, girls learned the many duties and skills they would need as homemakers when they grew up. Boys learned to be good hunters, fishermen, ballplayers, and warriors from their male relations, typically their mother's brothers.

Maturing

Choctaw children were usually named after an animal or an event associated with their birth. As they grew, they were given new names at special celebrations. These new names recognized a personal achievement or trait.

Boys became skilled at shooting rabbits and other small game, not only with bows and arrows but also with blowguns. Both girls and boys contributed food to their families through their hard work as hunters and gatherers. By the time they had become teenagers, they had learned all the skills they would need to support a family. Girls and boys were then considered adults who were ready to be married.

Marrying

The Choctaw deeply respected marriage, and most couples remained together for life. Young people usually chose their own mates. When a young man was attracted to a young woman, he waited for a time when she was alone gathering wood or doing some other task. He then approached her and tossed a small pebble in her direction. If she wished to be courted by him, she smiled. If not, she scowled. To declare his intentions, he might also enter her home and lay a handkerchief or hat on her bed. If she approved of him, she left the object there. If not, she removed it from her bed.

When two young people agreed to be married, they arranged a time and a place for the wedding. On the day of the wedding, the families of the couple arrived and stood about 100 yards (91 m) apart. The brothers of the bride approached the man and seated him on a blanket. The sisters of the bride then seated her next to the groom. Occasionally, as a joke, the woman would break away and pretend to flee from the man. She would then have to be pursued and returned to the blanket.

The bride's family placed a sack of bread next to her, and the groom's family set a bag of meat near him. The bread represented her role as a gatherer and gardener, and the meat symbolized his responsibilities as a hunter. The groom's family and friends then showered gifts on the bride—money, clothing, and household objects. Her relatives quickly gathered the gifts and shared them among themselves. The couple then rose and were considered husband and wife.

Everyone enjoyed a great feast, after which the couple either built their own home or lived with their parents.

Dying

When a person died, the body was dressed in special garments that had been passed down through generations of the family. Mourners then viewed the body. However, the deceased was not buried in these clothes. When a child died, people mourned for three months. If a parent died, the mourning lasted from six months to a year. During this painful time, women cut their hair. In the last three days of mourning, people wailed three times a day—at dawn, noon, and sundown. At the end of this time, mourners placed a wooden triangle near the entrance of their home.

The body was placed on a scaffold about 5 or 6 feet (1.5 to 1.8 m) above the ground. When the remains had decomposed, the bone picker, a painted and tattooed man or woman with long fingernails, scraped what was left of the flesh from the bones. As the mourners looked on, the scaffold was burned. The bones were placed in a basket and taken to a community building known as the bone house. The bone picker then hosted a feast in honor of the deceased. Several times a year, when the bone house became full, the bones were taken away and buried in an earthen mound. A large communal funeral was then held for everyone who had died during that time.

Rituals of Agriculture

In the summer and fall, women, children, and old people gathered many kinds of plants, fruits, and berries in tall grass baskets. Most of these foods were eaten fresh. They also harvested wild grapes, plums, persimmons, and crab apples and dried them for later use. The Choctaw also picked hickory nuts, pecans, beechnuts, and chestnuts, sources of food and oil. Women pounded the dried nuts into flour to use in breads, soups, and stews. They extracted oil from hickory nuts by parching, or roasting, them in a pot until they crumbled into pieces. Then they pounded the pieces into a meal about

These Choctaw men, women, and children are dressed mostly in Western clothing.

as fine as coffee grounds. The meal was boiled for an hour or so into a thin soup, and then the oil was strained out through a cloth. The oil could be used at once for seasoning foods or stored in containers for later use. Hickory oil kept well for a long time.

Like other tribes of the Southeast, the Choctaw were excellent farmers, and much of their food came from their fields. To prepare new fields for planting, the men first cleared the land by burning away the underbrush and small trees. Swinging stone axes, they girdled the large trees by chopping a circle around the trunks. The trees soon dropped their leaves and died. The women

Corn was an important crop to the Choctaw. It grew easily in the warm Southern climate and provided the tribes with important nutrients.

planted among them until the wood rotted and the trunks could be toppled and carried away.

Women planted the crops, which included corn, beans, squash, and sunflowers. They grew several varieties of beans for use in breads, soups, and stews. Sunflower seeds provided oil and flour for breadmaking. The women also did most of the everyday work of cultivating the crops. The men tended small plots of tobacco, which they traded or mixed with dried, crumbled sumac or sweet gum leaves and smoked. After they came into contact with Europeans, the Choctaw began to grow sweet potatoes and vegetables such as

The People and Culture of the Choctaw

cabbage, peas, onions, leeks, and garlic. Many people also began to raise poultry and hogs. However, corn, which grew well in the fertile soil and warm climate, remained the Choctaw's major food crop.

Before the corn was planted, the townspeople held a dance. Then, the women went to work in the field. With a pointed planting stick, they made holes in the hills of mounded soil and dropped in the hard kernels of corn. As the corn grew, the women hoed the weeds with a tool made of the shoulder blade of a buffalo, a flat stone, or a seashell attached to a wooden stick. As the ears ripened, the Choctaw built platforms near the fields and stationed young people there to scare away the crows and other hungry birds. At harvest time, everyone helped to bring in the corn, and dances, feasts, games, and other ceremonies were held. The Choctaw grew different kinds of corn to eat fresh, cook in stews, or pound into meal for making breads. Most of the corn and other crops were stored for the winter in community houses.

Women ground corn between two stones or with a wooden mortar and pestle. Early mortars consisted of a large stone or a wooden trough—a log with the side hollowed out. After European traders introduced metal axes and chisels, men made mortars by hollowing out part of a section of tree trunk. With a pestle—a wooden pole with a heavy club at one end—women pounded the hard kernels of corn. They also ground beans, sunflower seeds, acorns, hickory nuts, wild potatoes, and dried meat in the mortars. Hickory wood was preferred for mortars because it gave a nice flavor to

People ground up their food using a pestle and mortar.

the food. Oak and beech were also favored, but maple gave food an unpleasant taste.

Hunters and Fishermen

In the Choctaw Nation as well as other Native communities, gender roles were present, but none were superior to the other. Instead, they complemented each other. Skilled hunters and fishermen, for instance, were the perfect complement to gathering and gardening. Men and boys used bows and arrows to shoot deer, their principal quarry, along with bears and turkeys. They also hunted opossums, raccoons, otters, and beavers. Otters and beavers were shot with arrows,

The People and Culture of the Choctaw

then clubbed before the wounded animals could slip back into the water.

To craft a new bow, the men used hickory that had been cut in the fall and allowed to season through the winter. During the first warm days of spring, they carefully shaped the wood into a bow. They twisted rawhide for the bowstring. The Choctaw also used hickory for the arrows because this wood seldom warped and the shafts remained true. To make arrowheads, they chipped pieces of flint gathered from along Nanih Waiya Creek, Tallapoosa River, and other streams, or they used slivers of cane or bone. After the Choctaw began to deal with European traders, they fashioned pieces of steel into points.

Boys and men hunted rabbits, squirrels, birds, and other small game with a blowgun, or *uski lumpa*, made of a hollow cane about 7 feet (2 m) long. They shot darts, or *shumatti*, made of slivers of cane fletched with thistledown. The thistledown was carefully fitted so that the dart fitted snugly inside the blowgun. Both boys and men were experts at fitting a dart into the blowgun and taking careful aim. With a single, powerful breath of air, they could send the dart zipping through the blowgun and into the flesh of an unlucky animal with deadly speed and accuracy. After they acquired firearms, the Choctaw abandoned their blowguns and bows and arrows. Guns proved to be much more effective, especially in bringing down large panthers and bears in the thick cane of the swamps.

Unlike the neighboring Chickasaw, who hunted bears and other large game in communal hunts, the Choctaw usually hunted alone or in small groups.

They quietly stalked their prey through the forests and swamps, dense with thickets, brambles, and canebrakes. Even small boys wandered for miles, hunting with blowguns and bows and arrows, and returned home at night. Following landmarks—stumps, rocks, fallen trees, unusual bushes, and streams—they never got lost, and their parents never worried about them. Men often journeyed far from home to unfamiliar territory. They set up camp, hunted all day, yet found their way back to their camp in the evening. If a hunter shot a small animal, he carried it along with him. If he killed a deer or other large game, he headed in as straight a line as possible back to the town, breaking twigs to mark his path. By following the broken twigs, his wife then returned to the place with a small packhorse and brought the game back to the village. While she dressed the carcass and prepared a meal for him, he would sit quietly by the fire, smoking his pipe.

During the summer, the Choctaw hunted mainly squirrels and other small animals, while during the winter they pursued deer and bear. Men knew the ways of the animals and every sound in the forest. They were expert at calling deer and using the stuffed skins and antlered heads of the animals as decoys. Sometimes, hunting in pairs at night, one man would hold a torch, freezing a deer in its light, while his companion took aim.

The Choctaw used a variety of methods to catch trout, perch, suckers, and occasionally catfish. In rivers and lakes, they speared fish and shot them with bows and arrows. The arrows were fitted with barbed points and long strings so the fish could be retrieved. Men also placed fish traps of woven cane in the streams,

The People and Culture of the Choctaw

or they dragged the stream with a net woven from brush and vines. They tossed buckeyes, winterberries, or devil's-shoestrings into the still pools of creeks. Chemicals from these plants briefly stunned the fish, which could then be easily gathered. The Choctaw also caught saltwater fish, shrimp, crab, and oysters on the Gulf Coast, and hunted turtles.

Men used tools such as bows and arrows to hunt.

Families kept what fish and game they needed and shared the surplus with others in the town and sometimes with Choctaw in other regions. Meat from fish and game was either eaten fresh or dried for later meals. Fish and game were considered a sacred part of life, and nothing was to be wasted.

Cooking

Women prepared a variety of meals consisting of soups, stews, and breads. During the hunting seasons, the Choctaw had fresh meat to roast or boil. They also had domesticated birds and hogs, but these were raised to be traded and were seldom eaten. The pig was especially prized by the Choctaw.

Corn, a main ingredient in many dishes, was roasted, boiled, or baked. Women made bread with cornmeal and flour from dried beans and sunflower seeds. They moistened the mixture of dry ingredients with water, eggs, or hickory milk to form dough, which was shaped into loaves and baked. Boiled together in a broth, corn and beans made a nourishing meal. Vegetables and meats were added to enrich the soups and stews.

Hominy, or the inner part of a corn kernel, was made into a kind of porridge known today as grits. Popular hominy dishes included *tashlubona* and *tafula*, which is sometimes called *holhponi*. To make tashlubona, corn kernels were soaked in water to remove the hulls more easily. The hominy was then cooked with pork and salt. To make tafula, the kernels were cooked with beans and wood ashes.

One of the most popular dishes was *banaha*, which is similar to the tamale. The Choctaw also adapted new recipes such as *pashofa*, which is made with cracked corn (pearl hominy) and fresh pork. Today, favorite foods among the Choctaw include Indian tacos, or *hattak* tacos, made with ground beef, tomatoes, chili beans, cheddar cheese, seasonings, and other ingredients, served on fry bread. Corn fritters, or *pask alwasha tanchi*, which are made by deep-frying corn batter, are also enjoyed.

Clothes and Accessories

Choctaw women made all the clothing for their families. Traditionally, like other tribes of the Southeast, people wore garments made of tanned animal skins, usually deer hides. When the weather grew cold and when

The People and Culture of the Choctaw

RECIPE

BANAHA

INGREDIENTS

2 cups cornmeal

1 ½ cups boiling water

1 teaspoon baking soda

1 teaspoon salt

About 12 dried cornhusks

Thoroughly sift together cornmeal, baking soda, and salt. Add water. Mix with hands to form a firm dough. Shape portions of dough into oblong loaves, each about 3 inches long and 1 inch wide.

Briefly boil the cornhusks until they are soft and pliable. Wrap each small loaf in a husk. Tie the middle with strips of cornhusk. Carefully drop each banaha into a pot of boiling water. Cook for 30 to 40 minutes. Banaha tastes best when served hot.

A Choctaw woman wears a richly decorated dress, headband, and beads.

people went on journeys, everyone put on moccasins. Otherwise, they went barefoot.

In warm weather, boys and men wore only a **breechcloth**, a rectangular piece of **buckskin** drawn between the legs and tied with a belt around the waist

The People and Culture of the Choctaw

with flaps hanging over the front and back. They also wore buckskin shirts or shirts made from feathers woven into cords. During the cold winter months, they tied buckskin leggings to their belts with thongs and tucked them into their moccasins. Leggings were also tied just under the knees with a decorated garter, or belt.

Women wore skirts, usually made of buckskin. During the winter, they wore shawls of buckskin, woven feathers, or the inner bark of the mulberry tree. The shawls were fastened over the left shoulder. After contact with Europeans, the Choctaw traded for brightly colored cloth, which the women made into dresses. People often adorned their clothing with beads and ribbons. Men also traded for brass bells, which they strung on their legs below the knees.

Silver earrings made by a Choctaw member

Both men and women liked to wear jewelry—necklaces, bracelets, and earrings made from shells, bones, and stones. They also wore necklaces made of wooden beads as large as acorns or dyed chinquapin nuts. Sometimes, they strung winterberries or red haw berries to make necklaces. People often pierced their ears and noses and adorned themselves with ornaments made from bear claws.

Men plucked their beards, so they had no facial hair. Unlike other Southeastern tribes, both men and women wore their hair long. Men often wore feathers in their hair to indicate their rank and accomplishments. Using combs made of shells, bones, antlers, or copper, women usually wound their long hair into a roll tied at the back of their heads. They frequently wore bead ornaments or flowers in their hair.

Flattening the head was traditionally considered a mark of beauty among the Choctaw. Newborns were placed in a cradle and tilted back so that their weight rested on the crown. A bag of sand or other weight was then placed on the forehead. One traveler described the "head somewhat the form of a brick," with a high forehead "sloping off backwards."

Men and women painted designs on their faces in various colors, usually red, white, and black. When going to war, men painted themselves and the handles of their war clubs with the symbols of their clan. People also tattooed their faces and occasionally their shoulders. The tattoos told a person's age, marked the time when young men became warriors, and indicated position within the tribe. Tattoos usually consisted of figures of animals and plants along with complex symbols representing the person's clan and moiety.

Arts and Crafts

Choctaw women were especially skilled in weaving baskets of rich colors and striking patterns. Although baskets were made for everyday use, they were also prized for their beauty. Women gathered cane during the winter when it tended to be less brittle. They

The People and Culture of the Choctaw

stripped off the outside skin of the cane, the part to be used in the weaving, with a knife made especially for this task. They then soaked the strips of cane in water to make them more pliable. With these supple strips, they wove many kinds of baskets and utensils for storing goods, sifting flour, gathering wild plants, and harvesting crops.

Women often colored their finished baskets with a yellow dye obtained from puccoon roots that had been gathered in the fall. Other times, they used walnut hulls to obtain a brown dye and maple roots for a deep purple color. They boiled the roots to obtain the dye. The strips of cane were then coiled and boiled in a round pot filled with the dye.

Choctaw women wove baskets with unique designs. These are some examples of the baskets and designs they created.

The tradition of basketmaking flourished long after many of the Choctaw were removed to Oklahoma. The Mississippi Choctaw who evaded removal continued to make sturdy, colorful baskets. As recently as the 1930s, families walked the back roads to trade their finely crafted baskets for corn or bacon. At one time, all Choctaw girls learned the art of weaving baskets, and today many Choctaw women are highly skilled artisans. Choctaw baskets are now considered works of art. They are sold for high prices to tourists and collectors. Many baskets are also on display in museums.

Warring

Before they went to war, the Choctaw held a war dance known as the *pa´shi isht hila*. In the shadows of the forest evening, they kindled a great fire. Whooping and singing war songs, warriors danced in a circle around the blaze. Sparks from the crackling fire shot high into the branches of the trees overhead and into the gloom around them. The next day, the warriors broke camp and set off to enemy territory. They padded through the forest in small bands, one behind the other in a straight line. Each warrior tried to step quietly in the tracks of the one who walked before him, which made it difficult for enemies to estimate the number of men in the band. The last warrior in the line tried to cover the tracks to remove any evidence of their passage. During the journey, the warriors maintained a strict silence, communicating only by hand or head gestures or by softly imitating the cry of a wild animal.

With faces painted to strike terror in their foes, they advanced silently on the enemy camp or

This painting shows a Choctaw warrior named Kutteeotubbee.

village. Hidden by the deep green undergrowth, they approached in small parties. To wage a pitched battle in an open field, even against equal odds, was considered foolish. The Choctaw sought to outwit their enemy, which was considered a great and praiseworthy tactic. Relying on clever strategy and the advantage of surprise, they waited patiently for just the right time to mount their attack. The warriors then swept down on the unsuspecting village. It was considered a disgrace for the chief to be surpassed in daring by any of his warriors, and it was equally dishonorable for the warriors to be exceeded by their chief. So, the chief and the warriors competed fiercely among themselves to ignore danger and outdo one another in daring feats of heroism. After the attack, the warriors vanished into the forest, scattering in all directions in hope of eluding any pursuers, and regrouped at a previously arranged location miles away.

To become a warrior was the highest calling of a Choctaw man, and warriors who distinguished themselves in battle rose to become chiefs. Yet the Choctaw seldom went to war without a just cause— which was usually to avenge an attack or other wrong committed by their enemies.

Traveling and Trading

The Choctaw journeyed by foot over paths and trails, known as traces, that linked their towns. They also traveled along well-worn paths to visit the villages of other Southeastern tribes. To help travelers find their way through the dense forest, the routes were often marked with symbols painted on rocks or trees or with small earthen mounds. Running from the present-day city of Natchez, Mississippi, to Nashville, Tennessee, the Natchez Trace was the most important of these routes. For hundreds of years, the Choctaw used this route to trade among themselves and other Native peoples. Settlers also came to walk the Natchez Trace.

The People and Culture of the Choctaw

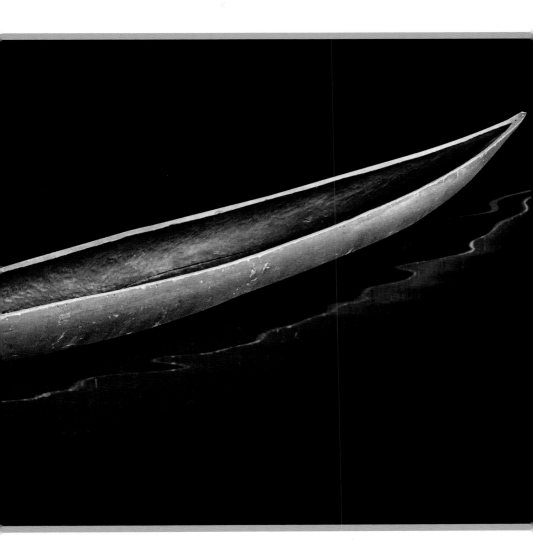

This drawing shows a dugout, popularly used by the Choctaw.

The Choctaw also traveled by canoe, paddling their graceful **dugouts** along the many rivers within their territory. They often ventured as far west as the Mississippi River and as far south as the Gulf of Mexico. To make a dugout canoe, men first chopped down a large tree using stone axes. They then carefully shaped the trunk, tapering each end so that the canoe would glide smoothly through the water. Finally, setting a row of small fires along the length of the trunk, they alternately burned and scraped out the inside wood with shells. Hollowing out a canoe was a long and arduous task, but a large vessel could carry twelve to fifteen people. Men also made rafts by lashing canes together. They used poles to push their rafts as they transported goods through swamps and other still waters.

The Choctaw often traded or shared goods with other towns of the tribe. Using a well-established network and a language based on Choctaw words, they also traded with the other tribes in the Southeast. Among the many items exchanged were bearskins, beaver pelts, buffalo robes, seashells, freshwater pearls, and copper. They traded surplus corn and other crops for these goods. The Choctaw were regarded as a thrifty people with good business sense who bargained well.

In the early 1700s, the French established colonies in what became the cities of New Orleans, Louisiana; Biloxi, Mississippi; and Mobile, Alabama. The Choctaw soon began to trade animal skins and other goods for the metal tools, guns, bags of flour, wool blankets, and cloth offered by these newcomers. Although the Choctaw strongly desired these useful items, they remained wary of the Europeans because of their previous mistreatment at the hands of the Spanish explorers led by Hernando de Soto.

Over time, the Choctaw adopted many European tools and practices. They began to use plows to prepare their fields and spinning wheels to make yarn. They learned how to raise domesticated livestock—cattle, pigs, chickens, and horses. They even developed a new breed of small horse, popularly known as the Choctaw pony, that proved to be very useful as a pack animal on hunting expeditions into the forest.

The Choctaw established trading posts at key locations. Some Choctaw became quite wealthy, especially after they learned the value of money as a medium of exchange.

In general, the Choctaw and the French got along. Some Choctaw women even married French traders. However, soon the mix of European and Americans settling on their land became too much. The Choctaw and other Native nations got caught up in conflict. In the 1700s and 1800s, a series of wars between the Choctaw and settlers disrupted trading relations and nearly tore apart the Choctaw Nation.

This statue depicts the Choctaw Turtle storyteller.

CHAPTER FOUR

BELIEFS OF THE CHOCTAW

The track of the Sun across the sky leaves its shining, eternal message illuminating, strengthening, warming ... all of us who are here it shows us we are not alone. We are yet alive. And this fire, our fire shall not die.

—Choctaw prayer

Just as the Choctaw had different rituals for stages of life, they had unique traditions concerning religion and belief. These traditions were challenged over the years by concepts of Christianity and other religions. However, some celebrations remain even to this day.

According to the Choctaw, the Sun is the supreme god, or Great Spirit.

The Great Spirit

The primary god, or Great Spirit, of the Choctaw was the Sun, which they called **Hushtahli**, from *hashi*, meaning "sun," and *tahli*, meaning "to complete an action." The term may also more accurately describe Great Spirit as "the governor of the world whose eye is the sun." Looking down upon the earth, the Sun had the power of life and death. Anyone on whom the Sun fixed his eye thrived, but as soon as the Sun turned away, a person died. The Choctaw also believed that the Sun offered a bright path in war. Leaders offered thanks to the Sun after every victory and prayed for a safe return to their homes.

However, the Choctaw believed that the Sun did not influence most daily activities. Having created the world and its inhabitants, including their laws, the Sun

The People and Culture of the Choctaw

returned above, and people could ask nothing more of him. Thus, in prosperous times, the Choctaw did not express gratitude and in hard times they did not call upon the Sun for relief. During droughts, they relied on rainmakers to work magic. Instead of worshipping the Sun, they lived in dread of his powers. The Choctaw also revered Fire, which closely resembled the Sun, and was considered his mate. They believed that the Sun and Fire constantly spoke with each other, and people were careful never to commit an offense in the presence of Fire. If they did, Fire would tell the Sun as quickly as he could move *ashatapa*, the length of his arms, in a futile attempt to escape punishment.

Other Spirits

The Choctaw believed in many other spirits—good and bad. These spirits waged an intense war within each person. The good spirits brought happiness and prosperity, while the bad spirits inflicted pain and misfortune. When a person enjoyed "good medicine," the good spirits were dominating this battle. During times of hardship or "bad medicine," bad spirits were controlling a person's fate. The presence of the spirits was made known through certain sights and sounds—a flock of birds exploding into flight, the wind sighing through the trees, the eerie *who-who* of an owl, and the distant, lonely howl of a wolf.

Like the other Southeastern tribes, the Choctaw also believed in a little man who lived in the thick forests. Some people believed there were several little men, but most thought there was just one impish character. Known as Bohpoli, meaning "Thrower," or Kwanoka´sha, meaning "Forest-Dweller," the little man was about 2 feet (0.6 m) tall. Mischievous but not malicious, Bohpoli loved to play tricks. He threw sticks or rocks at people and made strange noises in the woods. He especially liked to strike pine trees at night while people camped in the woods. Although Bohpoli lived secretly, hidden among the trees, Choctaw shamans claimed to have seen and spoken with him. They said that Bohpoli helped them to make medicines. It was believed that Bohpoli sometimes kidnapped a boy and revealed to him the secrets he needed to become a medicine man or shaman.

The Choctaw believed in other forest spirits as well. Kashehotapalo, who was part deer and part man, delighted in frightening hunters. Okwa Naholo (or Oka Nahullo), meaning "white people of the water," lived in deep pools. They had light skins like trout and occasionally snatched people whom they transformed into spirits like themselves. Hoklonote´she, an evil spirit who could assume any shape he wished, was able to read people's thoughts. Nalusa Falaya, or the Long Black Being, who resembled a man with small eyes and long, pointed ears, liked to scare hunters. Hashok Okwa Huiga, or Grass Water Drop, whose heart was only visible and then only at night, led astray anyone who looked upon him. The Choctaw also believed that Ishkitini, the horned owl, prowled at night, not only hunting animals but also people.

The Choctaw thought that many animals, especially owls, had supernatural powers. If an owl lighted on a tree near a house, it foretold a death in the family. If a screech owl, or *ofunlo*, called out in the night, it meant that a child younger than seven would die soon. The screech of a horned owl was considered a warning of sudden death or murder. The sapsucker, or *bishinik*, brought news—either good or bad. If the bird lit on a nearby tree early in the morning, this news would come before noon. If the bird arrived late at night, the news would come before morning. The Choctaw believed that chickens had been brought to them to offer warnings of danger. If a rooster crowed at an unusual time, it meant bad weather was on the way. If a rooster crowed after flying up to its roost, it meant trouble for the family. If a hen crowed, it foretold that the women in the area were about to have a disagreement.

Personal Spirits

The Choctaw believed that a person had two spirits: **shilombish** and **shilup**. The shilombish was one's outside spirit in life. After death, the shilombish remained on earth as a ghost. Wandering about its old haunts, especially at night, the shilombish often took the form of a fox or an owl and barked or screeched to frighten people and to foretell misfortune or even death. The shilup was an interior spirit that upon death journeyed to a happy place known as the land of ghosts. This afterworld had two parts, good and bad, separated by a mountain. Anyone who had committed a serious offense, such as murder or telling a lie that led to murder, leaving a pregnant wife, or even gossiping, was condemned to the bad area. In later years, the Choctaw came to believe that after a person died, the shilup had to walk a slippery log over a churning river. The shilup of a good person was able to cross and continue on its journey to the pleasant land. The shilup of a murderer or evildoer stumbled into the abyss and was condemned to wander in misery.

Religious Leaders and Medicine

The Choctaw had several classes of holy men and healers in a priestly order, including doctors, shamans, rainmakers, and fair-weather makers. Both men and women could become doctors, acquiring considerable knowledge about the many herbs and roots that were effective in treating physical illness and injury. For example, these doctors made wormseed into a medicine that children who had worms ate as a candy. Mayapple fruit was given to children as a purgative.

Cherries were thought to have healing abilities and so the Choctaw never cut down cherry trees.

The People and Culture of the Choctaw

Adults also imbibed a drink made from a very small amount of powdered mayapple root. Pottage pea, an onion-like root with a sweetish taste, was administered in cases of diarrhea. Modoc weed was used to treat weak stomachs, fainting spells, and nervous disorders. Wild cherry was considered one of the best medicines, especially for young girls, so these trees were never chopped down. The leaves or bark were boiled to make a tea that was considered a healthy tonic to purify the blood. The Choctaw also boiled pennywort leaves to make a broth for cleansing wounds. They boiled the leaves, stem, and bark of Sampson's snakeroot and wafted the steam over snakebites. Boneset was steamed to cause one to throw up in case of food poisoning. The Choctaw pounded the roots of rabbit tobacco and soaked the pulp in water to make a drink that relieved fever. Scurvy grass was used to clean teeth. Prickly ash relieved toothache when a small piece of bark or a poultice of powdered bark was put in the cavity.

Doctors often treated people through sweating. Wrapping themselves in several layers of blankets or retiring to a sweat lodge, the patient drank hot tea. Cures also included cold baths. To heal the afflicted, doctors also used dancing, songs, and prayer. A method of sucking away the illness was often employed.

Some men and women sought to obtain spiritual as well as healing powers. As priests and shamans, they drove out evil spirits, foretold the future, and undertook other feats that helped the people in their town. It was believed that a priest could influence the weather, bring rain or sunshine for the crops, and encourage fish and animals to allow themselves to be caught. A priest could also instill strength and courage in warriors and ballplayers. A person seeking to become a priest went alone into the forest to fast, meditate, and pray. For days, even weeks, in what became a long and weary ordeal, he sought to speak with the spirits—first lesser spirits and then the Great Spirit through whom he would obtain his extraordinary powers. Only a few men and occasionally women were able to achieve such deep spiritual communication. They became the religious leaders with the highest and most honored place in Choctaw society.

Changes

Encounters with Europeans brought many rapid changes to the Choctaw, including their religion, and many of these traditional beliefs were abandoned. By the mid-1800s, most Choctaw in Mississippi and Oklahoma had embraced Christianity. Many became ministers, and people said prayers and sang hymns at church services in the Choctaw language.

Celebrations and Ceremonies

Nearly every Choctaw town had a square or open place where people gathered for councils and celebrations. They held their most important feast, the **Green Corn Dance**, which lasted as long as five days, when the first green corn was harvested. At this time, the ears were ripe, but still tender, like the sweet corn eaten today. The Choctaw did not have as many festivals as other Southeastern tribes. However, they gathered for feasts and dances to heal a sick person

The Choctaw use feathers and bright colors to decorate their bodies during special rituals and celebrations.

or prepare for war. They also had dances when the fields were cleared in the spring and when the corn was planted. The Choctaw held a dance for young people, a scalp dance for victorious war parties, and a ball-game dance. Ceremonies varied from town to town.

The Choctaw had dances in which they wore masks that looked like the heads of the eagle, turkey, buffalo, bear, and alligator. The Eagle Dance was performed by twelve or sixteen men whose bodies were painted with white clay. Each man held an eagle tail and wore eagle feathers on his head. The men sat in rows of four, one behind the other. At the beat of the drum, four men sprang up and danced while squatting low around spears stuck into the ground. When they became exhausted, they retired to the back of the rows, and the next group of four men took their place in the dance.

These gatherings were full of poetry and music, dance and song. People painted their faces and dressed in their finest clothes. They wore belts of metal bells and loved the jingling sound that blended with the singing, the shaking of the rattles, and the rhythmic beating of the drum around which they moved. Begun about midmorning, the dances continued for the entire day. The musicians played rattles, cane flutes, and drums. To make a drum, the Choctaw used a section of hollowed-out tupelo gum or sometimes a cypress knee for the drum body. They stretched a piece of wet, pliable deerskin or bearskin over the top and held it in place with a hoop of hickory wood. Drumsticks were made of maple, poplar, or ash and had a knob on one end. Sometimes, the knobs were wrapped in cloth. However, musical instruments were secondary to the melodious blending of voices in song. After the dance, people sat down to a great feast to which the women contributed bread and the men brought game.

People also liked to come together to listen to stories, especially during the winters. Many of these stories recount the Choctaw's relations with the creatures of the earth and their struggles to provide for themselves. Here is a story about how two hunters brought corn to the people:

> Many moons ago, two Choctaw hunters were
> camped for the night on the swamp along
> a bend of the Alabama River. Having failed
> in their pursuit of game, the two hunters sat

The People and Culture of the Choctaw

Singers use many instruments during ceremonies. Today instruments such as drums are still used in celebrations and traditional dances.

Beliefs of the Choctaw

beside their fire with a hawk as their only food.

They thought of their hungry families who would be disappointed when they returned home with no game. They worried about the gloomy future of their people, if they could not provide meat for their wives and children. They roasted the hawk over the fire and were eating a poor and scanty meal when in the distance they heard a low, foreboding moan like the cooing of a dove.

The woeful moans broke the deep silence of the dark all around them. As the moon ascended in the sky, the moaning became more frequent and distinct. With wide eyes and pounding hearts, the hunters peered up and down the river, trying to ascertain the source of the melancholy sounds in the night. But only the banks of the river glittered in the moonlight against the murky waters.

Suddenly, a wondrously beautiful woman appeared in the distance. She was standing on a mound, illuminated in the moonlight of the forest. She wore a white gown and carried a wreath of flowers. Standing within a halo of light that gave her the appearance of a spirit, she beckoned them to approach her.

The two hunters believed that she was the Great Spirit of their nation and that the flowers were the spirits of loved ones who had passed from the earth to bloom in the land of the spirits. They came to her and offered to help her in any way possible.

She confessed to them that she was very hungry. Immediately, one of the hunters ran back to camp and brought her what was left of the roasted hawk. She gratefully accepted the hawk, but after eating a small portion, she handed it back to the hunters. She told them that she would remember their kindness and generosity when she returned to her home where she lived with her father, who was Shilup Chito Osh, a great spirit of the Choctaw people. The two hunters realized that she must be his daughter, Ohoyo Chisba Osh.

She told them when the next full moon came in midsummer they should meet her at the mound. Bidding them good-bye, she was at once borne away in a gentle wind.

The two hunters returned to their camp for the night. In the morning they went home but told no one about the encounter with Ohoyo Chisba Osh. It was to remain a secret between them.

At the full moon of midsummer, they quietly returned to the foot of the mound, but Ohoyo Chisba Osh was nowhere to be seen. Then, remembering that she had instructed them to come to the very spot where she had been standing, they ascended the mound. They found the top of the mound covered with a strange plant, each with a single stalk and blade-like leaves. This plant yielded a wonderful food. The Choctaw have since cultivated this plant in the fields around their towns. They named the plant *tanchi*, or corn, and thereafter, even when game was scarce, they no longer went hungry.

Fun and Leisure

The Choctaw enjoyed many games, especially stickball, or *ishtaboli*, which is still played avidly today. The modern game of lacrosse is based on stickball. This fiercely contested game was played between neighboring towns or tribes or between teams chosen from within a town. Matches were often played to settle disputes, and wagers were placed on the outcome. Any number of players could take part in the contest. The playing field, or *hitoka*, was about 200 to 300 yards (600 to 900 feet) long with a goal at each end. Each goal consisted of the halves of split logs planted upright in the ground about 6 feet (1.8 m) apart with the split side facing the field and a horizontal pole connecting them.

Opponents handled a deerskin ball with two 3-foot-long (0.9-m-long) *kapucha*, or hickory sticks. One end was trimmed flat and bent into a small, oblong hoop. Thongs of raccoon skin were laced over the hoop to form a webbed cup for catching, carrying, and flinging the ball. The object was to scoop up the ball and hit the uprights of the team's goal and to keep the opponent team from scoring. Players could not touch the ball with their hands, but otherwise there were no rules. The number of points needed to win the match, often as many as one hundred, was agreed upon before the players took to the field.

Matches were usually planned well in advance. As runners traveled to villages over the countryside, they carried bundles of sticks to help calculate the date. Each day one stick was thrown away until only one stick remained, which meant that the eve of the game had at last arrived. Coming from all directions, people gathered at the playing field and held a great celebration. People sang as women danced in two lines and the men danced around their goals, shaking their playing sticks. Through the night, the shaman of each side called on the spirits to aid their players. Old men who had been chosen to serve as referees quietly smoked as they awaited the upcoming game.

The next day the referees assumed their places on the field. The players then assembled, wearing only breechcloths, their bare bodies strikingly painted. To start the game, one of the referees threw the ball into the middle of the field, and the men sprinted after it. Competitors played with grace, strength, and remarkable agility. They displayed great skill in handling and passing the ball as they roughly jostled each other. Running, leaping, and dodging each other, they raced with the ball or tried with their sticks to snatch it away from an opponent. When a player scored a goal, he and his teammates brazenly mocked their opponents by gobbling like wild turkeys. Throughout the match, the shamans urgently called upon all their spiritual powers to come to the aid of their side.

The Choctaw used these items to play stickball.

Stickball games were hard-fought battles, with much at stake. Players were often seriously injured, and sometimes killed, in the heat of competition. People often lost all their possessions in bets. However, at the end of the game, no matter who won, there was seldom any bad feeling or poor sportsmanship. After the men had finished their stickball match, men and women often competed in a similar game. This game was played with a larger ball, but it could be caught and carried in one's hands.

The Choctaw played another game, called *ulth chuppih* or *alhchahpi*, in which round stones about 6 inches (15.2 centimeters) in diameter were rolled over smooth ground. Players threw poles at the stones, trying to strike the opponent's stone or prevent him

The People and Culture of the Choctaw

from hitting one's own stone by deflecting his pole in midair. In the game *naki lohmi*, a small object was tucked under an article of clothing, and the opponent tried to guess where it was hidden. They enjoyed a dice game in which they threw kernels of white corn charred black on one side and guessed how many kernels of one color or the other would be turned up. Women also played a game similar to jacks in which they threw a small ball in the air and tried to pick up a stick or other object before the ball hit the ground.

Although all these games were played by other Southeastern tribes, the Choctaw tended to engage in them more eagerly than the others. Whereas other tribes were more deeply involved in religious ceremonies, the Choctaw thoroughly enjoyed many social gatherings, sports, and games.

Over generations, the Choctaw have thrived and continue to be an essential part of the Native community despite hardships, especially in the 1800s and 1900s. Their ability to adapt to surroundings and their dedication to social activities helped them face these difficulties and prevail.

The lives of many Native Americans changed with the arrival of Europeans.

CHAPTER FIVE

*Do not take up
the warpath without
a just cause and
honest purpose.*

—Pushmataha,
Choctaw leader

OVERCOMING HARDSHIPS

From the 1500s to the twentieth century, Native communities around North America have endured drastic upheaval to their lifestyles and traditions. Many believe there was a desire to essentially eradicate any notion of Native life in North America. Many Native Americans, including the Choctaw, were forced from their homelands to lands far away. Some settlers targeted and killed Native people, while the US government set up rules for Native Americans and schools that taught Native children different beliefs. This is known as genocide. Indeed, many cultures that encountered Native Americans saw them as different and enforced rules that made it difficult, or nearly impossible, for them to live in their Native communities and continue their deeply rooted traditions and beliefs.

Europeans Arrive

The Choctaw encountered Hernando de Soto in 1540 when he journeyed through southeastern North America in search of wealth. He yearned to discover a civilization that had as much gold and silver as did the Incas. In the Choctaw town of Moma Bina, he demanded that the women and men carry his goods. When Chief Tuscaloosa refused, the Spanish and Choctaw clashed. Both the Spaniards' baggage train and the town were burned. Having never seen horses before, the Choctaw were terrified of the Spanish warhorses and suffered many casualties. However, the warriors were armed with bows and arrows and inflicted considerable damage on de Soto's expedition. After resting, the Spanish continued through Choctaw territory without further conflict.

The Choctaw did not again encounter Europeans until the French claimed the huge territory of Louisiana in 1699 and established the cities of Mobile, in what is now Alabama, and New Orleans in the early 1700s. The Choctaw formed a close yet frequently strained relationship with their neighbors to the south. Through their alliance with the French, the Choctaw were drawn into costly conflicts with other tribes, especially the Natchez and Chickasaw. During the 1730s, they and the French fought in a war of extermination against the Natchez. The Natchez who survived the warfare

Native American communities traded European settlers furs in exchange for weapons, food, and other tools.

fled to the Chickasaw. Although the Choctaw and the Chickasaw were closely related, the Choctaw allied with the French and fought the Chickasaw until the French departed from North America in 1763.

Since the 1730s, the Choctaw had also been trading with British merchants from the Carolinas. The British offered better-quality goods at a lower price than did the French. The British had long been trading with the Chickasaws, and the French were afraid that they would next lose the Choctaw as trading partners. The French and British competition for Choctaw trade led to a violent conflict in which Red Shoes, a great Okla Falaya chief, became the prominent leader. As a young man, he fought with the French against the Chickasaws. However, after a Frenchman attacked one of his wives in 1734, Red Shoes sided with the British. He encouraged trade and peaceful relations with his new allies and the Chickasaw. Enraged by Red Shoes's actions, Pierre de Rigaud, the French governor of Louisiana, demanded that the Choctaw kill Red Shoes to prove their loyalty to the French king. In 1748, as Red Shoes was returning from a trading journey, warriors ambushed and murdered the great leader. His assassination sparked a civil war among the Choctaw that came to be known as the Choctaw Revolt.

This bitter dispute, which raged from 1748 to 1750, had a devastating effect on Choctaw society. Entire villages were destroyed. The Choctaw gradually realized they were killing themselves because of the colonial powers. The factions at last agreed to peace. The Choctaw were thereafter able to maintain a tense relationship with both the British and the French. After

The People and Culture of the Choctaw

the French left North America, the Choctaw were approached by the Spanish, who sought them as allies. Through their dealings with European powers, the Choctaw learned to be skilled and cautious diplomats. This experience later helped them in negotiations with the United States.

During the American Revolution (1775–1783), the Choctaw supported the rebelling colonists and provided scouts for several generals, including George Washington. In 1786, they made their first treaty with the young United States—a statement of peace and friendship. In 1801, they allowed the federal government to build a road through their territory. Thereafter, Americans not only passed through Choctaw lands but also began to settle on homesteads around their towns. Settlers began to demand more land, and President Thomas Jefferson suggested that Native peoples of the Southeast give up their lands and move west. In 1805, during negotiations for what became known as the Treaty of Mount Dexter, the United States began to pressure the Choctaw to surrender their homeland and move to territory west of the Mississippi River.

In spite of these pressures, the Choctaw tried to maintain peaceful relations with the United States. In 1811, the great Shawnee leader Tecumseh visited the southern tribes and encouraged the Choctaw to join his alliance of tribes against the United States. However, the Choctaw chief Pushmataha, who was known to be a persuasive orator, convinced his people not to join Tecumseh. Pushmataha also eloquently spoke at the councils of the Creek and urged them to be loyal to the United States. He succeeded in keeping the Creek, except for a belligerent faction known as the Red Sticks, from allying with Tecumseh. In the War of 1812, the Choctaw, led by Pushmataha, allied with the United States against the British. Made a lieutenant colonel in the United States Army under General Andrew Jackson, Pushmataha led several hundred warriors against the Red Sticks, and then the British at the Battle of New Orleans. Later, these Choctaw warriors joined Jackson's campaign against the Seminole in Florida.

Difficult Times

In 1816, despite their loyalty and sacrifice in these military campaigns, the Choctaw were forced to sign another treaty with the United States. During negotiations in this treaty, the government again demanded that the Choctaw give up a large portion of their land. By 1817, enough settlers had moved into the territory to establish the state of Mississippi. These people sought to take the fertile lands of the Choctaw. In the treaty of 1820, the Choctaw agreed to trade a substantial part of their land for a large tract west of the Mississippi River, in the area designated as Indian Territory. In 1823, a Choctaw delegation led by Peter Pitchlynn traveled to Indian Territory to inspect the lands. In 1830, after Andrew Jackson became president, the United States demanded that the Choctaw relinquish the rest of their land in Mississippi and move to the West. Choctaw leaders, including Pitchlynn, David Folsom, Greenwood LeFlore, and Mushalatubbee, were forced to sign an agreement that became known as the Treaty of Dancing Rabbit Creek.

Treaty of Dancing Rabbit Creek, September 1830

(Seating of Leaders)

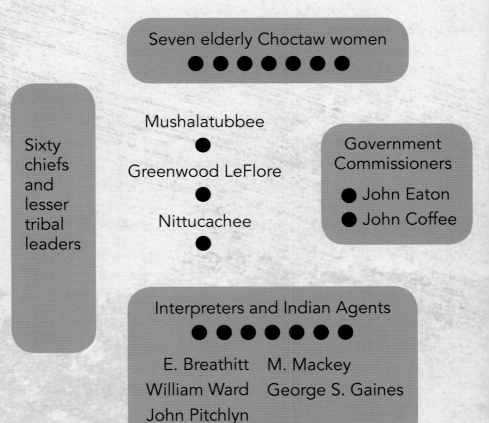

Seven elderly Choctaw women
● ● ● ● ● ● ●

Mushalatubbee
●

Greenwood LeFlore
●

Nittucachee
●

Sixty chiefs and lesser tribal leaders

Government Commissioners
● John Eaton
● John Coffee

Interpreters and Indian Agents
● ● ● ● ● ● ●

E. Breathitt   M. Mackey
William Ward   George S. Gaines
John Pitchlyn

Audience: Choctaw Nation and Guests

Between 6,000 and 12,000, mostly Choctaw and some Americans; men, women, and children.

LeFlore helped to create a treaty whose terms were favorable to the Choctaw, but he could not prevent their removal.

According to terms of the treaty, the Choctaw were to be relocated. Badly planned, the three brutal marches of 1831 to 1834 became a national tragedy. In the first march, supervised by the Bureau of Indian Affairs, the government decided that costs were too high—even though many Choctaw paid for their own removal from the sale of their lands. To save money, the army, which managed the next two marches in 1832 and 1834, cut rations and blankets. With little food and no protection from the bitter weather, 2,500 people—mostly old people and many children—died of starvation, illness, or exposure in these marches that became known as the Trail of Tears. By 1834, about 11,500 people had moved to Indian Territory in present-day Oklahoma. The Choctaw were the first people to be relocated as an entire nation. Other tribes, notably the Cherokee, soon suffered their own Trail of Tears as they, too, were moved to lands west of the Mississippi River. Throughout the remainder of the nineteenth century, Choctaw people continued to move from Mississippi to tribal lands in Indian Territory, often at the encouragement of tribal leaders in Oklahoma.

As many as six thousand Choctaw refused to be relocated and remained in Mississippi. In accordance with the Treaty of Dancing Rabbit Creek, they could have individual parcels of land totaling 640 acres (259 ha) for each head of household, 320 acres (130 ha) for each child over ten years old, and 160 acres (65 ha) for younger children. However, only

The People and Culture of the Choctaw

This illustration shows harsh conditions the Choctaw and other Native American groups endured on the Trail of Tears.

sixty-nine heads of household were ever allowed to own land in Mississippi. Having lost everything, the Choctaw became squatters on what had been their own land or hid out in the swamps. In 1918, the United States government at last gave the Choctaw a small reservation near Philadelphia, Mississippi. Over time, they became the Mississippi Band of Choctaw Indians, a federally recognized tribe with its own lands in east-central Mississippi.

The Choctaw who had moved to Indian Territory gradually adapted after the painful tragedy of the removal and formed a government. Leaders wrote a constitution based on the Constitution of the United States that was adopted by the Choctaw government. Under the leadership of Peter Pitchlynn, the Choctaw established an effective government, built an excellent school system, and developed a strong, stable economy. Within a generation, the Choctaw had begun to flourish in their new home. However, in 1866, the federal government forced the Choctaw to sell their western lands as punishment for having been allied with the Confederacy in the Civil War. In the treaty, a railroad right-of-way was also granted through Choctaw territory. Like the wagon road that had passed earlier through their Mississippi lands, the railroad brought large numbers of settlers into the region. By 1890 the Choctaw were again overwhelmed by a flood of settlers. In the Treaty of Dancing Rabbit Creek of 1830, the US government had promised the Choctaw that they could keep their land forever. However, in the 1890s, they and other Native peoples in Oklahoma were again forced to surrender their land and move into smaller areas. In the Dawes Act of 1893, the individual members of each nation, including the Choctaw, were required to accept an **allotment** of land. In the Atoka Agreement of 1897, the Choctaw relinquished all their lands. The Choctaw Nation was dissolved entirely in 1907 when Oklahoma became a state.

The People and Culture of the Choctaw

A child learns the Choctaw language from her uncle.

Learning the Language

Choctaw belongs to the **Muskogean** language family, widely spoken in the Southeast. Among the so-called **Five Civilized Tribes** (Choctaw, Chickasaw, Creek, Seminole, and Cherokee), only Cherokee is not a Muskogean language. All of these Southeastern tribes used a simplified version of the Choctaw language when they met for trade. Choctaw is very similar to Chickasaw, and is closely related to the language of the Creeks and Seminoles. Since 1988, the Choctaw Nation has offered classes to their community and the wider world population, encouraging others through the use of social media and the internet to explore and appreciate the Choctaw language. To learn more, visit their website: https://www.choctawnation.com.

The following sampling of words is based primarily on *A Dictionary of the Choctaw Language* compiled by Cyrus Byington in 1915. Choctaw is a complex language, but the following key and examples should be helpful for basic pronunciation of words.

Vowels are generally pronounced as follows:

a	as in father
a	as in tub
e	as in met
i	as in pin
o	as in go
u	as in full

Consonants are generally pronounced as in English. The letter *s* is pronounced as in sir, never as in his.

Paired vowels, known as diphthongs, are pronounced as follows:

ai	as in pine
au	as in now

Nasalized vowels are indicated by ´.

Unlike many other Native peoples, most Choctaw still speak their native language. Following are some everyday words used by the Choctaw.

Expressions

aiokpanchi	welcome
a´ya	farewell

a´h, akat, i´, u´kah, yau	yes
ahah achi	no

People

ishki, ishki toba, i´hhukni	aunt
alla nakni	boy
anakfi	brother
a´ki, apokni	cousin
chuka achafa	family
a´ki	father
hatak ikhana	friend
alla tek	girl
hatak	man
chiske	mother
ibaiyi	nephew
ibitek	niece
antek	sister
a´ki	uncle
hatak ohoyo, ohoyo	woman

Parts of the Body

ibbak, shakba	arm
haknip	chest
haksobish, tanch ampi	ear
ibbak i´shu´kani	elbow
chiluk, nishkin	eye
apaknali	face
ibbak ushi	finger
iyi	foot
ibbak	hand

anumpa nushkobo	head
chu´kash	heart
iyi´ kalaha	knee
api, iyapi	leg
itakha	mouth
ibichilu, ibishakni	nose
fulap, tahchi	shoulder

Natural World

ahoshonti	cloud
lukfi	earth
bokko, bunto	mound
umba	rain
bok, chuli	river
shutik	sky
hashi	sun
api, iti	tree
okfa	valley
fichak	water

Animals

nita	bear
hushi	bird
yannash	buffalo
isi	deer
ipaf, ofi, ofi puta	dog
ha´khobak	duck
o´ssi	eagle
ushi	egg
isi chito	elk
nani	fish

chula	fox
shukatti	frog
isuba	horse
alhpoa, nukoa	pet
chukfi, chukfi luma	rabbit
sintullo	rattlesnake
koni	skunk
fani	squirrel

Language is very important to Native cultures across North America and the preservation of those languages is valued among all of them. The Choctaw are immeasurably fortunate to have so many of its people speaking their traditional tongue.

The Choctaw Nation displays its seal in Durant, Oklahoma, in July 2015.

CHAPTER SIX

They'll know we are Choctaw by our heart.

—Current Choctaw campaign

THE NATION'S PRESENCE NOW

Over many decades, the Choctaw regrouped and adapted to their new surroundings. However, it was not an easy task. Today, the Choctaw have separate governments in two different states. The two federally recognized tribes are the Mississippi Band of Choctaw Indians and the Choctaw Nation of Oklahoma. The Choctaw in both Mississippi and Oklahoma are working to ensure prosperity for themselves and future generations of their people.

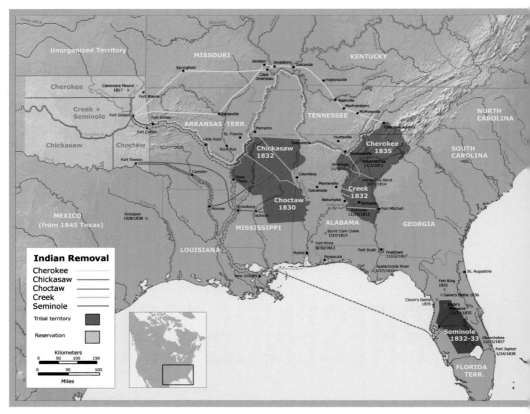

This map outlines the different routes each tribe took on the Trail of Tears and the areas in which they settled.

Building a New Society in a New Land

Allotment and other changes proved tragic for the Choctaw in Oklahoma. Often, they were cheated out of their small farms. Tribal members did not receive payment for the sale of public lands until 1920 and the sale of mineral rights until 1949.

Until 1948, the US president appointed the chief of the Oklahoma Choctaw. This chief was responsible for administering tribal affairs. In the 1970s, due to the efforts of Chief Hollis E. Roberts, the Choctaw became self-governing and achieved recognition as the Choctaw Nation of Oklahoma. In 1975, Roberts acquired a historic building from Presbyterian College in Durant, Oklahoma, to use as tribal headquarters. Six years later, in 1981, the US government recognized the Choctaw Constitution of 1860. On July 9, 1983, the Choctaw people ratified the constitution.

Ignored by the federal government and living at the margins of society, the Choctaw in Mississippi retained their language and traditional culture. In 1917, an influenza epidemic swept through Mississippi, killing one in five Choctaw people. A year later, in 1918, the US Bureau of Indian Affairs opened the Choctaw Indian Agency in Philadelphia, Mississippi, to assist the people living in the area. The agency formed schools for Choctaw children and started to purchase small parcels of land in 1920. By 1944, the agency had acquired 16,000 acres (6,474 ha). The Mississippi Choctaw continued to struggle until 1969 when Chief Philip Martin secured a grant of $560,000 from the Economic Development Administration to build an industrial park known as Chahta. Packard's Electric Division of General Motors became the first client, followed by other major corporations such as Ford, Xerox, and AT&T. This industrial park grew to include many other businesses. In 2015, the Mississippi Band of Choctaw Indians celebrated their seventieth anniversary of self-government.

Today, the Choctaw Nation of Oklahoma manages many social, economic, and health services, as well as job-training programs. Its website, https://www.choctawnation.com, features a detailed history of the Choctaw Nation, key information about the Choctaw

The Choctaw Nation Capitol Museum and Judicial Department features many exhibits with detailed historical information about the Choctaw tribe.

The People and Culture of the Choctaw

government and recent accomplishments, and a Choctaw TV YouTube channel.

Recent Times

Over the past two decades, the Choctaw in both Oklahoma and Mississippi have embarked on several successful business ventures. The Mississippi Choctaw have attracted major industries to the reservation. After an industrial park was established in the Pearl River community in 1973, General Motors Corporation opened the Chahta Wire Harness Enterprise, which assembles electrical components for automobiles. The American Greeting Card Corporation soon followed with a plant on the reservation, and the Oxford Investment Company began making automobile radio speakers at the Choctaw Electronics Enterprise. In 2002, Chahta Enterprise opened a commercial laundry operation, and in 2014 they opened a metal fabrication operation. Today Chahta Enterprise is among Mississippi's top ten employers.

The Mississippi Choctaw have also been engaged in a construction boom that began in 1965 when the Choctaw Housing Authority built the first of over two hundred modern homes on the reservation. In 1969, the Chahta Development Company, which constructs and remodels homes, offices, and buildings, was established on the reservation. The Choctaw Health Center, a forty-three-bed hospital, opened in 1976. Since then, new homes and schools have been built in communities scattered all over the reservation, along with many new tribal buildings.

In 1994, the Mississippi Band of Choctaw Indians, as the tribe is now officially known, opened the Silver Star Casino. In 2001, groundbreaking took place for the Golden Moon Casino, which is located across the street. Although some tribal members opposed gambling, profits were carefully invested in educational and social services in the community. The Choctaw Nation of Oklahoma, meanwhile, has many different casinos around Southeastern Oklahoma.

Inside the Golden Moon Casino, owned and operated by the Choctaw

The People and Culture of the Choctaw

Community Interactions

Over the years, the Oklahoma Choctaw have established community centers and clinics in small towns throughout the reservation. Through the efforts of the Choctaw Housing Authority, thousands of people have been provided with modern, low-cost homes. The Choctaw now operate hospitals, schools, restaurants, tourist centers, and travel plazas throughout Mississippi and Oklahoma.

Other initiatives in Oklahoma include the restoration of the buildings and grounds of the historic Choctaw Council at Tushkahoma, located in the heart of the reservation. In 2015, the nation began the Choctaw Nation Next Step Initiative, which seeks "to assist Tribal Members reach the next step of self-sustainment through supplemental food vouchers as well as financial fitness and healthy living." A state-of-the-nation report also said as many as 1,300 new jobs had been created during that year.

Overall, the federally recognized Choctaw communities continue the traditions of their ancestors, through perseverance, hard work, and annual ceremonies. They have survived amidst terrible hardship and loss, and have rebuilt their lives, adapting to the world around them as their ancestors before them.

Phyliss J. Anderson is sworn in as Choctaw chief in October 2011.

*A starving man will
eat with wolves.*

—Choctaw proverb

FACES
OF THE
CHOCTAW

Throughout history, members of the Choctaw people have contributed to politics, art, science, and so much more. Here are some of the activists, thinkers, artists, and more who have helped shape American society.

Owanah Anderson (1926–), a social activist, was born in Choctaw County, Oklahoma. She went to school in Boswell, Oklahoma, where she was valedictorian of her high school class. She received a scholarship to the University of Oklahoma, where she studied journalism.

During the late 1970s, Anderson became an advocate for the rights of Native Americans and women. In 1977, she served as a chairperson of the Texas delegation to the Houston Women's Conference. From 1977 to 1980, she served on the Committee on Rights and Responsibilities of Women established by the US Department of Health, Education, and Welfare. In 1979, she also founded the Ohoyo Resource Center, which assisted women with educational and employment opportunities. In 1982, Anderson edited *Ohoyo One Thousand*, a publication that profiled more than one thousand prominent Native American women. *Ohoyo* means "woman" in Choctaw. After the center closed in 1983, Anderson moved to New York City, where she became chairperson of the National Committee on Indian Affairs of the Episcopal Church. She has served on the board of directors of the Association for American Indian Affairs and as project director for the National Women's Development Program.

Phyliss J. Anderson (1961–), chief, was born on January 1, 1961. One of seven daughters, Anderson grew up in a tribal frame home in Leake County, Mississippi. She gained much of her strength and hardworking nature by following the example of her mother. In 2003, she became a tribal council representative, where she served for eight years as secretary-treasurer. She was elected the first female chief of the Mississippi Band of Choctaw Indians in 2011. Five years later, in March 2016, US president Barack Obama appointed Anderson to serve on the National Advisory Council for Indian Education.

David Folsom (1791–1847), Choctaw leader, made his home near present-day Starkville, Mississippi. Along with Peter Pitchlynn, he was a strong advocate of education among the Choctaw and encouraged Presbyterian, Methodist, and Baptist missionaries to establish churches in Choctaw communities. In 1824, Folsom went to Washington, DC, to discuss Choctaw removal with federal officials. In 1826, Folsom became the first leader of the Choctaw's three governmental districts. Along with Greenwood LeFlore, he resisted land cessions and removal. When removal became inevitable, he worked hard to negotiate the best possible agreement for his people. In 1830, he reluctantly signed the Treaty of Dancing Rabbit Creek. After he had relocated to Indian Territory, Folsom settled on a farm south of the town of Caddo.

Rosella Hightower (1920–2008), ballerina and dance teacher, was born in Ardmore, Oklahoma. When she was still an infant, her family moved to Kansas City, Missouri, where she began to study ballet at an early age. After several years of study, she was asked by ballet master Leonide Massine to join the Ballet Russe de Monte Carlo in southern France. For two years she danced under Massine, then returned to

Rosella Hightower dances with James Urbain.

The People and Culture of the Choctaw

the United States in 1942 where she joined the Ballet Theatre, which was later renamed the American Ballet Theatre. She then joined the Original Ballet Russe and toured North and South America until 1947. She returned to the Grand Ballet de Monte Carlo, later known as the Grand Ballet du Marquis de Cuevas. She became prima ballerina and achieved international fame for her dancing until 1962. She danced with Rudolf Nureyev and on television and in movies.

In 1962, Hightower founded her own school, the Center for Classical Dance, in Cannes, France. In 1967, she returned to the United States to take part in the critically acclaimed ballet *The Four Moons*, with three other Native American ballerinas from Oklahoma. She continued to dance until 1977, after which she devoted herself to teaching and directing dance productions. In 1975, the French government honored her with the Chevalier de la Legion d'Honneur. She received the Officier de la Legion d'Honneur in 1988 and the Grand Prix national de danse in 1990.

Hightower died in her home in Cannes, France, in 2008. She was eighty-eight, and it is believed that she suffered a series of strokes.

Clara Sue Kidwell (1941–), author, educator, and historian, was born in Tahlequah, Oklahoma, to a Choctaw father and Chippewa mother. She was raised by her grandmother in Muskogee, Oklahoma, while her parents worked. She received a bachelor's degree at the University of Oklahoma. She later earned a master's degree and a PhD in the history of science. She taught history at several colleges and universities before becoming an associate professor of Native American studies at the University of California at Berkeley in 1974. She has published several articles and books about Native Americans, including *The Choctaws: A Critical Bibliography*. In 1993, Kidwell became assistant director of cultural resources at the National Museum of the American Indian of the Smithsonian Institution in Washington, DC. She worked at the University of Oklahoma for a time, and then conceptualized and became director of the American Indian Center (AIC) at the University of North Carolina in 2007. She retired four years later, in 2011.

Portrait of Greenwood LeFlore

Greenwood LeFlore (1800–1865), leader and plantation owner, was the son of Nancy Cravat, a Choctaw woman, and a French trapper named Louis LeFlore. By the mid-1820s, LeFlore owned large tracts of land and had become one of the wealthiest Choctaw at the time. In 1828, LeFlore was named by Thomas McKenney, US Superintendent of Indian Affairs, to lead a Choctaw expedition to Indian Territory. The purpose of this trip was to inspect lands for the Choctaw who were to be moved there. However, as principal chief of the two northern Choctaw districts, LeFlore joined with David Folsom and opposed the

Choctaw leader Mushalatubbee, who had agreed to removal from Mississippi. Holding out for the most favorable terms, LeFlore eventually suggested a compromise to Andrew Jackson. In 1830, this plan formed the basis of the Treaty of Dancing Rabbit Creek. LeFlore himself never relocated. Remaining in Mississippi, he lived at his plantation along the Yazoo River and was later elected to the state legislature.

Linda Lomahaftewa (1947–), artist and educator of Hopi and Choctaw descent, was born in Phoenix, Arizona. Influenced by her creative parents and

brothers, she attended the Institute of American Indian Arts in Santa Fe, New Mexico, in 1962. After receiving her high school diploma there, she earned bachelor's and master's degrees in art at the San Francisco Art Institute. Her work has been included in

Linda Lomahaftewa

numerous exhibitions in the United States and around the world and is displayed in many galleries and museums, including the Southern Plains Indian Museum in Anadarko, Oklahoma. She has taught at several colleges and universities. Since 1974, Lomahaftewa has been a drawing and painting instructor at the Institute of American Indian Arts. She has received many awards for her work.

Phil Lucas (1942–2007), film producer, director, writer, and actor, was born and raised in Phoenix, Arizona. After attending Phoenix Community College from 1960 to 1961, he traveled around the United States as a guitarist and folk singer. Returning to Arizona, he attended Mesa Community College, then Western Washington University, where he completed a bachelor's degree in communications in 1970. After a brief career in advertising, in 1974 he began to work at the United Indians of All Tribes Foundation in Seattle and to make films. In 1979, Lucas wrote, coproduced, and codirected a five-part Public Broadcasting Service (PBS) series about stereotypes of Native Americans in movies and on television. In 1980, he established the Phil Lucas Production Company and wrote, produced, and directed distinguished films and television programs. Among his successes are *Beyond Hunting and Fishing*, a 1989 television program about Native people in British Columbia, and a fifteen-part series entitled *Native Americans: Images of Realities* that he created for the Canadian Knowledge Network the same year. In 1993, he coproduced *Broken Chain* for Turner Network Television. This dramatic film addresses the relationship of the Iroquois Confederacy with Great

Britain and the American colonies. Lucas died in 2007 in Bellevue, Washington.

Mushalatubbee (1770–1838), Choctaw chief, led a group of warriors that joined General Andrew Jackson in the Creek War of 1813–1814. As chief of a tribal district, Mushalatubbee took part in many negotiations with soldiers and government officials. Over the years, he signed treaties at the Choctaw Trading House in 1816; the Treaty Ground in 1820; Washington, DC, in 1825; and Dancing Rabbit Creek in 1830. In the last treaty, he agreed to surrender Choctaw lands in Mississippi and move to Indian Territory—in opposition to Greenwood LeFlore and David Folsom. Not long after he moved to Indian Territory with his people, Mushalatubbee died of smallpox.

Peter Pitchlynn (1806–1881), principal chief, was born at the village of Hushookwa, Mississippi, the son of John Pitchlynn, an interpreter for Pushmataha and federal officials, and Sophia Folsom, who came from one of the most influential families among the Choctaw. As he grew up, Pitchlynn observed someone writing a letter and became determined to receive an education. When he returned from his first term at school, Pitchlynn became upset when he saw his people negotiating an unfair treaty. In protest, he refused to shake the hand of General Andrew Jackson when he met him. Pitchlynn continued his education at an academy in Columbia, Tennessee, and Nashville University, where he graduated.

This painting of Peter Pitchylnn was created in 1834.

Settling on a farm, Pitchlynn married Rhoda Folsom. Becoming involved in tribal politics, he was elected to the Choctaw Council in 1824. He and David Folsom advocated the establishment of five English-language schools. In 1828, Pitchlynn joined a delegation that went to Indian Territory to inspect land for Choctaw removal. Realizing that removal could not be prevented, Pitchlynn negotiated hard to obtain the most suitable lands for his people and other favorable terms in the Treaty of Dancing Rabbit Creek, which he signed in 1830.

After the Choctaw removal was complete in 1834, Pitchlynn established a farm on the Arkansas River. He also played a major role in reorganizing the tribe and establishing schools in the Choctaw's new home in Oklahoma. Often traveling to Washington, DC, Pitchlynn addressed the president and Congressional committees. In 1860, he was elected principal chief of the Choctaw in Oklahoma. During the Civil War, Pitchlynn remained neutral, although three of his sons fought with the Confederacy. After the war, he spent most of his time in Washington, DC, where he persistently lobbied for compensation for the lands lost by his people.

After his first wife died, Pitchlynn married Caroline Lombardy in 1869. He became a Freemason and joined the Lutheran Church. He was acquainted with many of the most notable people of the day, including Henry Clay and Charles Dickens.

Pushmataha (Apushmataha, Oak Tree) (1764–1824), Choctaw leader and orator, was born along the Noxubee Creek in Mississippi. Pushmataha claimed that he had no parents and that he had sprung from an oak tree struck by lightning. As a young man, he distinguished himself as a courageous warrior in campaigns against the Osage and Caddo. In 1805, he became a chief and signed the Treaty of Mount Dexter in which Choctaw lands had to be given up. When Shawnee leader Tecumseh sought the support of the Choctaw and other southern tribes, Pushmataha

A portrait of Pushmataha

persuasively spoke against the alliance. In the Creek War of 1813–1814, he led a band of five hundred warriors allied with General Andrew Jackson. At the Battle of Horseshoe Bend, Pushmataha and his men played a key role in defeating the Creek traditionalists, known as Red Sticks, led by William Weatherford. In recognition of his service, Pushmataha was named a brigadier general.

In the years after the war, Pushmataha skillfully negotiated treaties in 1816 and 1820 to minimize the land cessions. He strongly advocated and supported education for Choctaw children and invested tribal funds and his own money in a system of learning for his people. In 1824, he became alarmed by further demands for Choctaw land. Pushmataha traveled to Washington, DC, where he lobbied President James Monroe and met the Marquis de Lafayette. During his visit to Washington, Pushmataha fell ill with a throat infection and died. He was buried in the Congressional Cemetery in Washington, DC, with full military honors.

Allen Wright (Kilahote, Let's Kindle a Fire) (1825–1885), leader, was born along the Yajnukui River in Mississippi. When he was just seven years old, Wright was relocated to Indian Territory with his family. However, his mother died just before removal, and most of his family passed away a few years after Wright's arrival in Oklahoma. Wright was left with just one sister when Cyrus Kingsbury, a Presbyterian minister, took an interest in him. Kingsbury gave him the name Allen Wright and sent him to missionary schools. Wright later attended school in New York, graduating from Union College in 1852 and Union Theological Seminary in 1855. He had mastered not only English but also Greek, Latin, and Hebrew. He married Harriet Newell Mitchell, a missionary from Ohio, with whom he had eight children.

In 1856, Wright was ordained into the Presbyterian Church. He began to work among his people and became deeply involved in many tribal issues. He was elected to the Choctaw house of representatives and the senate. He later became treasurer for the tribe. After the Civil War, he served as principal chief for two terms, from 1866 to 1870. In 1866, he suggested the name *Okla-humma*, meaning "Red People" for Indian

Territory. In 1907, Oklahoma became a state. During the 1870s and 1880s, Wright translated many works, including the Chickasaw constitution and laws, into English. In 1880, his Choctaw dictionary was published under the title *Chahta Leksikon*. Wright died at Foggy Depot, Oklahoma, where he is buried near his home.

Muriel H. Wright (1889–1975), historian, was born in the Choctaw Nation in Indian Territory. Her father was a physician whose family included several prominent Choctaw leaders, and her mother was a teacher of English and Scottish descent. Her grandfather was Allen Wright, who served as principal chief of the Choctaw Nation from 1866 to 1870.

After attending local schools, Wright went to Wheaton College in Norton, Massachusetts, in 1906, where she excelled in academics. Two years later, when her father was chosen to represent the Choctaw in negotiations with the US government, she moved to Washington, DC, with her family. Wright soon went back to Oklahoma to assist in establishing a school system. In 1911, she received a teaching degree from East Central State Normal School, then embarked on a successful career as a high school teacher, coach, and principal.

In the 1920s, she began to concentrate on historical research and writing. She wrote a number of articles, then published a significant four-volume work entitled *Oklahoma: A History of the State and Its People* in 1929. In 1943, she became editor of the *Chronicles of Oklahoma*, the journal of the Oklahoma Historical

Society, and held this position for thirty years. Much of her research dealt with the Choctaw and other Native Americans in Oklahoma. She published *A Guide to the Indian Tribes of Oklahoma* in 1951. Wright also held a number of positions in Choctaw tribal government, including secretary and cofounder of the Choctaw Advisory Council. Among her many awards was an honorary doctorate from the University of Oklahoma. Shortly before her death, the North American Women's Association named her the "outstanding Indian woman of the twentieth century."

These are just some of the most memorable members of the Choctaw who have made important contributions to both American and Choctaw societies.

CHRONOLOGY

1540 The Choctaw make contact with Europeans when they encounter Spanish explorer Hernando de Soto.

1699 The French claim of Louisiana includes Choctaw territory.

1729 French traders meet with Choctaw leaders, offer gifts, and request Choctaw help in fighting the Natchez.

late 1700s American settlers move onto Choctaw land.

1781 The Choctaw sign their first treaty with the United States, establishing the borders of their territory.

1800 The Choctaw have already lost much of their land in Mississippi.

1803 President Thomas Jefferson acquires from France for $15 million a vast tract of land west of the Mississippi River. Known as the Louisiana Purchase, the area includes what became known as Indian Territory.

1820 The Choctaw are forced to trade more of their land for territory west of the Mississippi River.

1830 Under President Andrew Jackson, the US Congress passes the Indian Removal Act. In the Treaty of Dancing Rabbit Creek, signed on September 27, the Choctaw are forced to surrender the rest of their ancestral land, totaling over 10 million acres (4 million hectares).

1831 The Choctaw begin their journey along the Trail of Tears from Mississippi to Indian Territory. By the end of the removal in 1834, twenty-five hundred people—mostly children and the elderly—have died.

1834 End of the main migration to Oklahoma.

1855 US government officials recognize the Choctaw and Chickasaw of Oklahoma as separate tribes.

1893 Congress approves the president's decision to dissolve the Five Civilized Tribes, including the Choctaw, through land allotment.

1898 Congress passes the Curtis Act, which leads to the loss of more Choctaw lands in Oklahoma.

1906 Congress passes legislation that makes tribal governments illegal, including those of Choctaw tribes in Mississippi and Oklahoma.

1907 Oklahoma becomes a state.

1910 Only 1,235 Choctaw people remain in Mississippi.

1917 A flu epidemic ravages the Choctaw of Mississippi.

1918 US government acknowledges the existence of several Choctaw communities in Mississippi when the Bureau of Indian Affairs creates the Choctaw Indian Agency in Philadelphia, Mississippi. Choctaw language is used as a code during World War I.

1934 The Indian Reorganization Act, which allows greater independence for Native Americans, is accepted by the Mississippi and Oklahoma Choctaw.

1945 The Mississippi Band of Choctaw Indians is recognized as a tribe by the US Congress.

1964 Congress passes the Civil Rights Act, which prohibits discrimination in employment, housing, and education. Choctaw Central High School, the Mississippi Choctaw's only high school, is built.

1969 The Choctaw Industrial Enterprises and an industrial park are established in Mississippi.

1975 The Indian Self-Determination Act allows Native Americans to develop their own tribal governments.

1979 The Mississippi Choctaw, under Chief Philip Martin, open the first of five industrial plants owned and operated by the tribe.

1983 The 1860 Choctaw constitution is ratified, becoming the law for members of the Choctaw Nation of Oklahoma.

1994 A hotel and casino are opened on the reservation of the Mississippi band of Choctaw.

2000 The Mississippi Band of Choctaw Indians, one of the top ten employers in the state, operates more than fifteen business enterprises with $375 million in annual sales.

2002 Chahta Enterprises starts commercial laundry operation.

2011 Phyliss J. Anderson becomes first female chief of the Mississippi Band of Choctaw Indians.

2014 Chahta Enterprises starts metal fabrication operation.

2015 The Mississippi Band of Choctaw Indians celebrate seventy years of sovereignty; the Choctaw Nation of Oklahoma starts the Choctaw Nation Next Step Initiative.

GLOSSARY

allotment Federal policy, starting in 1887, in which reservations were divided and parcels of land were distributed to individual Native Americans.

breechcloth A cloth or skin worn between the legs and around the hips; also called breechclout.

buckskin Deer hide softened by tanning.

Chata Traditional name for the Choctaw.

Choctaw Native American people, who traditionally lived in what became eastern Alabama, east-central and south-central Mississippi, and a sliver of Louisiana along the south border of Mississippi. Many Choctaw now live in Oklahoma.

clan Members of a large family group who trace their descent from a common ancestor.

dugout A type of canoe made from a tree trunk.

Five Civilized Tribes Informal alliance of Choctaw, Creek, Chickasaw, Cherokee, and Seminole tribes formed in 1859 to preserve tribal identity. The term "civilized" refers to their adoption of many Euro-American customs.

Green Corn Dance Most important Choctaw celebration of thanksgiving, forgiveness, and purification, held each year when the corn has ripened.

Hushtahli Choctaw word for the sun, believed to be the creator of the world.

iksa Choctaw name for clan.

Indian Territory Region in the south-central United States, including most of what is now Oklahoma, where the government relocated numerous Native American tribes.

matrilineal Tracing descent through the mother's side of the family.

Mingo Choctaw district chief.

mound Large, rounded hill made by early Native American as a burial place or as a base for a public building.

Muskogean Group of related languages spoken by the majority of Native American peoples living in the Southeast (also Muskhogean).

Nanih Waiya Sacred earthen mound believed to be the place of origin for the Choctaw people; also name of the first Choctaw council house in Indian Territory.

shilombish Spirit or ghost of a person that remains on earth after the person's death.

shilup Spirit or ghost of a person that has journeyed to the afterworld.

BIBLIOGRAPHY

Akers, Donna. *Culture and Customs of the Choctaw Indians.* Westport, CT: Greenwood Publishing Group, 2013.

Birchfield, D. L. *The Encyclopedia of North American Indians.* New York: Marshall Cavendish, 1997.

Cushman, H. B., and Angie Debo. *History of the Choctaw, Chickasaw, and Natchez Indians.* Norman, OK: University of Oklahoma Press, 1999.

Dawson, Imogene, and Cyrus Byington. *English to Choctaw Chata Dictionary.* Oklahoma City, OK: Holitopa, 1995.

Ethridge, Robbie. *From Chicaza to Chickasaw: The European Invasion and the Transformation of the Mississippian World, 1540-1715.* Chapel Hill, NC: University of North Carolina Press, 2010.

Mould, Tom. *Choctaw Tales.* Jackson, MS: University Press of Mississippi, 2004.

O'Brien, Greg. *Choctaws in a Revolutionary Age, 1750–1830.* Lincoln, NE: University of Nebraska Press, 2002.

Perdue, Theda, and Michael D. Green. *The Columbia Guide to American Indians of the Southeast.* New York: Columbia University Press, 2001.

FURTHER INFORMATION

Want to know more about the Choctaw? Check out these websites, videos, and organizations.

Websites

Choctaw Fact Sheet

http://www.bigorrin.org/choctaw_kids.htm

Read quick and easy facts about the Choctaw.

Choctaw Nation

https://www.choctawnation.com

This is the official website for the Choctaw Nation in Oklahoma. Learn about the Choctaw tribe's history and what life in the tribe is like today.

Mississippi Band of Choctaw Indians

http://www.choctaw.org

This is the official website for the Mississippi Band of Choctaw Indians.

Videos

Choctaw Nation OK

https://www.youtube.com/user/ChoctawNationVideo

Visit the Choctaw Nation of Oklahoma's YouTube channel to learn more about the language, culture, and heritage of the Choctaw people.

Choctaw Social Dancing: Choctaw Days 2013

https://www.youtube.com/watch?v=aOe9Z5R7Xd8

This clip from 2013 shows Choctaw dancers performing traditional social dances.

Crash Course US History: Age of Jackson

https://www.youtube.com/watch?v=beN4qE-e5O8

This video explains the era in which the Trail of Tears occurred under Andrew Jackson.

Mississippi Band of Choctaw Indians YouTube Channel

https://www.youtube.com/user/MBCI2013

Explore more about the Mississippi Band of Choctaw Indians by visiting their YouTube channel. There are many videos offering insight into the tribe's activities today.

Preserving the Choctaw Language

https://www.youtube.com/watch?v=3AyEWdTZOu8

This news segment explains how the Choctaw language runs the risk of dying out and how people are trying to preserve it.

Organizations

Choctaw Nation of Oklahoma
PO Box 1210
Durant, OK 74702-1210
(800) 522-6170
https://www.choctawnation.com

Jena Band of Choctaw Indians
PO Drawer 1367
Jena, LA 71342
(318) 992-2717
http://www.jenachoctaw.org

Mississippi Band of Choctaw Indians
PO Box 6010—Choctaw Branch
Philadelphia, MS 39350
(601) 656-5251
http://www.choctaw.org

Mowa Band of Choctaw Indians
PO Box 268
McIntosh, AL 36553
(334) 944-2243

INDEX

Page numbers in **boldface** are illustrations. Entries in **boldface** are glossary terms.

The People and Culture of the Choctaw

ABOUT THE AUTHORS

Samantha Nephew is a writer, activist, and community organizer, and is a member of the Seneca Nation of Indians (Deer Clan). Nephew is a graduate of Buffalo State College and Saint Bonaventure University and is working on her master's degree in public administration. She aims to continue working in her hometown community to create a socially and racially just life. She lives in Buffalo, New York, with her husband and two cats.

Raymond Bial has published more than eighty books—most of them photography books—during his career. His photo-essays for children include *Corn Belt Harvest*, *Amish Home*, *Frontier Home*, *The Underground Railroad*, *Portrait of a Farm Family*, *Cajun Home*, and *Where Lincoln Walked*.

As with his other work, Bial's deep feeling for his subjects is evident in both the text and illustrations. He travels to tribal cultural centers, photographing homes, artifacts, and surroundings and learning firsthand about the national lifeways of these peoples.

The emeritus director of a small college library in the Midwest, he lives with his wife and three children in Urbana, Illinois.